Twenty-nine

Poems on motherhood

Annie Ridout

For my mother, Julia

POEMS

01 I'VE JUST HAD A BABY
02 NOURISHMENT
03 THE THING IS
04 LOCHIA
05 THE EGG TIMER
06 THE FOURTH TRIMESTER
07 WHAT I WANT FOR YOU
08 GIVE HER BACK
09 MY BALL OF WOOL
10 THE MILKMAID
11 I'M A BETTER MOTHER THAN YOU
12 BRAND NEW BABY
13 TO MOTHERHOOD
14 IN TIME
15 WHITE FEATHER
16 MY HEART BROKE
17 PARANOID
18 IN BED
19 CHERISH EVERY MOMENT
20 PREGNANCY
21 IF
22 A MOTHER'S LIFE
23 BREASTFEEDING
24 THE TEARS OF 'WHAT IF'
25 JUST ANOTHER MANIC MOTHER
26 RAISING A BOY, AS A FEMINIST
27 BUT I WANTED A BABY
28 ME-TIME
29 NEW MOTHERHOOD, ONCE AGAIN

A document of gratitude and love

I'VE JUST HAD A BABY

I've just had a baby -
don't expect too much of me.
Invite me, but don't be annoyed if I say no.
For days, weeks, months.
I'll come when I can; when we're ready.
If you ask to visit and I hesitate,
please take that as a polite "no" (not yet).
But if I'm indecisive, gentle persuasion might be just what I need.
A quick visit, a cup of tea, talking about the world outside of my cocoon.
Company is important but so is rest.
I might appear selfish but I need to be:
right now, it's about me, my baby and my body.
If I push myself to please other people
I'll break down in both body and mind.
I need time, love, care, nurturing, support, understanding.
No negativity, judgement or expectation.
I've just had a baby.

NOURISHMENT

My sister gave me home-baked soda bread to dip in soup.
She also cooked the soup; it was creamy fennel and almond.
My mum came round and made a hearty chicken casserole
with yoghurt and brown rice and broccoli and green beans.
One friend baked gooey brownies, while another made tiffin.
And butternut squash tart, pasta sauce, granola, buckwheat salad.
My mother-in-law sent handmade chocolates, a friend delivered truffles,
we were plied with trifle, cupcakes and mini blackberry and
apple crumbles.
This food - whether it was baked or bought - felt like the
sweetest gesture;
a spoonful of thought, a slice of kindness, a little pot of love.

THE THING IS

I know you want to hold him
but he only wants me.
He only needs me.
When we're apart, he wakes and
desperately suckles because he
knows he'll be reunited with me.
"He's looking for a feed,
shall I pass him back?"
Well, yes, because only I can feed him.
But when he's back in my arms
he doesn't always drink the milk.
Sometimes, he falls back into a deep sleep –
he's safe; he's home.
Or he'll wrap his lips around my
nipple and stay like that:
not drawing out the milk, just attached.
Either way, he isn't wriggling or writhing.
He never cries when he's on me.
You see, the thing is:
he only wants and needs his mum.

LOCHIA

The baby came out and then you did:
in streams and clots and leaks.
A reminder that my baby had lived inside me
but you were all that remained.
Flushing through me, gushing out of me –
staining, splashing, smeared.
He pushed out, so pure.
You fall out, so dirty.
I show him off: he's on display.
I hide you from everyone's view.
The pads you fill are wrapped in tissue;
the knickers you ruin are thrown in the bin.
You are the remains of life inside me;
the last new life that will ever live inside me.
Once you're all cleared out – we're done.

THE EGG TIMER

This morning you leaned in to
kiss me
and Joni
and told me you felt like
my love
for you
is an egg timer and it's
run out
of sand.

After birth:

Belly bulging
legs buckling
hands shaking
baby howling.

Eyes watery
(actually: crying)
body bruised.
Why is the midwife scowling?

Day three:

Lochia flooding
womb contracting
fingers swollen
nipples bleeding.

Toddler tantrums
craving sugar
needing sleep.
Is the baby feeding?

Day seven:

Nipples healing
baby sleeping
Kegels working
body moving.

Toddler happy
belly shrinking
baby's growing.
Things are improving.

Day twenty-eight:

Calm home
baby smiling
toddler chatting
feeling better.

Sleeping
(together – me and baby)
brain functioning.
"No phase lasts forever."

Three months:
(Projected)

Sleeping through
feeding happily
toddler chirpy
oxytocin flowing.

Chaos over
hormones calming
order returned
the love is growing.

WHAT I WANT FOR YOU

I want you to live until you're ninety
and spend your years gazing up at the sky –
marvelling at the beauty of the setting sun,
transfixed by the movement of the clouds.

I want you to run into the crashing waves
and dip your head under the sea –
to splash and swim when the tide is in
and taste tangy sea salt on your tongue.

I want you to go off on adventures:
climb trees and find secret, hidden paths,
skip through wildflower meadows
and build dens out of branches, twigs and leaves.

I want you to use all your senses
to enhance your experience of this world,
to fill your ears with music and dance freely;
to savour sweet and spicy tastes and scents.

But most of all I want you to be smiling,
as you carve your own, unique path
lined with everything that makes you feel inspired
and awake and alive – and never tired.

GIVE HER BACK

She's three days old
and we're still bound
by an invisible cord.
You creep into our nest
to poach my chick
and hold her, as if she's yours.
Hours pass by
and I yearn for her touch
but you cruelly keep her trapped.
So I stretch my arms
to reach for my baby
and you begrudgingly
give
her
back.

MY BALL OF WOOL

I am the needle, with you as my thread;
separate beings but where I go, you're led.
In those early days, when you were curled up small,
I'd wrap you up in blankets, or muslin to keep you cool.
You were complex and compact, like tightly wound yarn,
and each cry required fixing, so I learned to darn.
We were bonded – and bonding – every waking hour;
you'd wail for my body when I was in the shower
and you'd yearn for my milk as I closed my eyes to sleep
but when nestled near my breast, I wouldn't hear a peep.
You could say we're in a bubble – but it's more a ball of wool
that will slowly be unravelled: you're the thread and I'm your spool.
I will guide you like a needle, keep you grounded like a bobbin,
let you run, explore, be free –
but keep you safe and bound to me.

THE MILKMAID

My milk comes in and
leaks white streams of
sustenance that my
baby doesn't catch.
And when he does feed,
the opposite breast
pours and sprays and
bobbles up around the
areola; at the end of the
milk ducts.
Soon, it evens out as
my baby tells my body
how much milk he needs -
through his feeds -
and the flow becomes steady
and the leaks dry up.
He feeds solely from my body for
six months.
My half-year as a milkmaid.

I'M A BETTER MOTHER THAN YOU

She's definitely too hot, put this on her.
She's freezing cold, wrap her up.
She's not at all hungry, she's tired.
You feed her too much, that's enough.

She's totally bored, she's restless.
She's over-stimulated, leave her be.
She'll be fine up there on her own.
I know what's best so listen to me.

Leave her crying, that's what I did –
and look at my kids, they're fine!
If you do everything just like I did,
you'll have perfect children like mine.

Close all the doors and the windows.
Open everything so there's a draught coming through.
You should take my advice and remember:
I'm a better mother than you.

BRAND NEW BABY

My baby's brand new,
fresh out of the womb,
like a present that's just been unwrapped.
And I want to hold him;
enjoy him –
not pass him around the room.
He's mine to keep close,
and protect from the world
he's not bothered by anyone else.
He knows my smell and the
sound of my voice -
so forgive me for being bold.
But if you ask to hold him,
I may shake my head
and tell you he's fine where he is.
It's like the umbilical cord's still intact
so for now,
I'll hold him instead.

TO MOTHERHOOD

Let's raise a glass to motherhood,
as we step into this role.
Let's celebrate this wondrous change -
beginning to unfold.
Let's recognise the graft and need for
gruelling analysis.
Let's not forget how significant
our contribution is.
Let's focus on the good times as they
drive us through the bad.
Let's note the joyous moments that
we hopefully all have.
Let's remember, though, it is okay to
find it bloody tiring.
And in those moments, remember that it
ends; we'll be retiring -
as one day they'll be all grown up and
out there on their own.
And then we'll wait, impatiently
for our children to come home.

IN TIME

When there's one, the love is focused;
it's all ploughed into that child.
When another's born, what happens –
does the love dilute or grow?
Another baby crying out for
your time and body and touch –
and yet there's still the older child
wanting and needing you, too.
And so you look for ways to keep both
children feeling loved.
You stretch, contort and balloon your heart
until there's enough to go round.
And in time, the children learn to love each
other, just like they love you.
And then you feel less pressure to be
everything to both.

WHITE FEATHER

I was bathing under the Sicilian sky
when a white feather floated down and caught my eye.
"It's an omen!" I exclaimed, and from then on I knew
that the following month I'd be carrying you.

Reproduction is science and we know how it works –
but there's an element of mystery too.
And so even those who'd normally damn the spiritual world
might suddenly notice 'signs' coming through.

When we try to nurture nature – to make it go our way –
we realise the magnanimity of this quest.
Because the earth; its energy and our chemistry
will be manipulated by neither wit nor zest.

Both fans of superstition and the non-believing mass
can grow anxious and so open their eyes wide
to any indication of things going their way –
appearing as cryptic symbols; in disguise.

So your conception was marked by a falling fluffy feather
and now I'm desperate to see your face and to hear your baby blether.
That's why I took great solace in the petal that just fell
from a bunch of pure white roses – it's a sign, I can tell.

MY HEART BROKE

The baby was newborn, laid on the floor,
and the toddler bolted over.
He tried to jump over the baby but he
didn't quite make the leap.
He landed – heavily, harmfully – on his
tiny brother's shoulder. And the
screams from both my boys shattered my
fragile heart into fragments.
The baby wailed in pain and I didn't
know what damage was done.
My big boy cried out in guilt; disbelief –
and his pain was arguably worse.
After checking the baby for injury,
I pulled his brother in under my wing
and both boys wept into my bosom,
their disparate pain flowing out in tears.
I shook with shock and held them close
until all our anguish subsided,
then we moved through the day,
as if nothing had happened,
but all left with a wound to heal.

PARANOID

Paranoid
Paranoid
Paranoid
Paranoid
Paranoid
Paranoid
– that's what you say I am.

IN BED

Staring into each other's eyes,
arms and legs twisted and looped.
The warmth of our torsos and heat of our hearts,
light up the darkened room.

Your eyelids drop, you slip into sleep –
and I'm left, still gazing at you;
wondering how you'll change over time,
as the years pass by and you grow.

I imagine us lying in a bed in Paris,
having roamed and coffee-d and dined –
again eyeing your face, as your breathing slows
and wondering if, in yours, I see mine.

In this dream, I can see that your face-shape has changed;
matured, cheekbones defined.
And I think back to this night, right now,
and wonder where the years have gone.

But for now, we're here, just you and me –
so safe, entwined – wrapped in love.
And I decide to focus on here and now
and let the future come when it comes.

They say the early years of motherhood whizz by
so to cherish every moment.
But you don't have to.
Because there will be days your baby cries non-stop,
or writhes around with wind.
And homemade meals your toddler carelessly
tips straight in the bin.
There will be tantrums so loud and furious
that you end up crying, too.
And sleepless nights of sickness where you
all have your heads down the loo.
There will hopefully also be smiles and laughter and
coos and tiny toes –
but this isn't the entirety of motherhood,
as anyone who's done it knows.
So cherish the cherish-able moments and
let the rest ebb and flow.
Because motherhood is like a river;
we can't always choose where it goes.

PREGNANCY

It makes me fat
and swell
and smell
and stretch
and ache
and tired.

It makes me slow
and leak
and burn
and wait
and fret
and wired.

But then I remember holding my newborn
daughter in my arms,
I loved her as soon as she entered the world;
I was instantly, utterly charmed.
I tell her that she made it feel like Christmas every day.
And I'd been given this gift of her to cherish in every way.
And then I had her brother and I
looked into his face. And saw that he was
new again; and required a different pace.
Again, the love was rushing and the challenges usurped with joy –
and I got to learn the differences between a girl and boy.
So now, as I grow bigger and wait to
meet my number three,
I try to let aches and pains and gripes wash over me.
Because I know as summer ends, we get to start again:
we meet our third and final child and that's where pregnancy ends.

IF

If you're ill,
don't touch my baby.
If you're dirty,
wash your hands.
If you want to hold him,
ask me.
But if I say no,
understand.
'cause he's young
and weak
and vulnerable;
he's only just been born.
And he's mine to protect
from illness and
danger;
to keep safe and
well and
warm.

A MOTHER'S LIFE

You might look at my life and see
lattes and playdates,
late afternoon wine-drinking and
slow mornings with the kids.

But behind this veneer sits
anxiety about their past, present and future.

"Did I breastfeed them too long –
or not long enough?"

"Is she ok at nursery –
or should she still be with me?"

"Do I treat him differently,
because he's a boy?"

"I left them to cry; to teach them 'self-settling' –
has this caused them damage or helped them to sleep?"

Don't judge a mother by the buggy or
clothes or rules or her temper,
whether she works full-time or is 'just' a mother.
She'll already be questioning herself quite enough.

BREASTFEEDING

The baby's out. Will she breastfeed?
She will; she roots and suckles and
colostrum drips into her
miniature mouth and we've done it:
we're breastfeeding.
Will she want another feed, though?
Yes, she does. She's hungry –
she feeds every half an hour.
Someone says: the feeds are short.
Oh. I thought I was doing a good job.
I get mastitis and need antibiotics.
I carry on feeding her but it hurts.
It hurts so badly.
Like being stabbed in the breast.
Someone says: it was all going so well;
you were like Mother Nature.
And I think:
Am I not now?
We continue with the breastfeeding.
She's fourteen months.
I feel proud. And sad.
But I'd like another baby and my
periods haven't returned.
A year later, we have a son.
I'm on the operating table,
about to be cut open.
But I ask to push once more and miraculously, he emerges.
I'm shaking. I find it hard to hold him.
He doesn't want to breastfeed.
But then later, he does.
His lips are puckered and soon it hurts.
My nipples bleed.
I cry with the pain.
At night, I dread the murmurs that mean he wants a feed.

But we get through it.
A bout of mastitis.
Antibiotics.
And then we're off;
he loves breastfeeding.
I wonder how we're ever going to stop.
But at fourteen months, we do.
I wean him off to have another baby.
A year later, he's born.
He latches and suckles.
Then he sleeps through the night.
I ask the midwife if I should wake him.
No, she says, let him sleep.
In the morning, he's still sleepy.
She helps me to wake him and
shoves my nipple in his mouth.
He starts to suck. He stops. And then
later that day, he's stripped to be checked.
He wants me. He cries.
He comes to me. He latches.
He sucks and feeds and feeds.
At home, he feeds and feeds some more.
I remember how still you have to be,
as a new mum.
All the breastfeeding.
But he's my last baby and I
treasure the closeness we have as he
comes to me for milk and comfort and we
sit or lie together, joined.
Lips to nipple.
Tiny hand pawing my breast.
His small frame curled into mine.
Just thirteen months to go, and then I'll
never breastfeed again.

THE TEARS OF 'WHAT IF'

At first, the tears stemmed from panic:
what's happening; will they keep him alive?
And then they were tears of guilt:
will it be my fault, if he doesn't survive?
Next, they were tears of gratitude;
for the NHS care he received.
From now on, I'll well up with tears of 'what if' –
but they won't fall; they'll be dried by relief.

JUST ANOTHER MANIC MOTHER

Look at me! Look at my babe!
We're wonderful, we're fine!
I'm chilled and coping and loving it –
I'm relishing every moment.

She's a gem by day, an angel by night –
she's perfect in every way.
She never cries, not really –
(except when hungry, tired, cold, hot, scared, bored, windy, stuck, hurt).

I never feel angry, I never get bored;
she brought purpose to my life.
Our happy family just smiles and laughs –
days out are utterly perfect.

You might look at us disbelievingly,
but what you see is the absolute truth:
a faultless family, the perfect posse –
I'm coping, I'm winning, I'm great.

RAISING A BOY, AS A FEMINIST

It was easy having a daughter,
because I knew just what to say:
"You can do anything you want to;
nothing will get in your way.
Well, there may be some tricky obstacles –
but you can kick them to the side.
Take up all the space that you can in the world –
you never have to hide."

It's harder having a son, because
he already knows his place –
it's up at the front, at the head of the table
it's winning without having to chase.
He'll be offered the jobs that a woman could do –
and told it's because he's best.
But it could be because he won't leave to give birth,
or request equal pay – and the rest...

And so my son needs to learn to be canny,
to treat girls and boys the same:
whether friend or foe or competitor –
we're all equal (well, that's the aim).
When men in power deride his sisters
for virtue of having a womb –
I'll teach him to rise up in solidarity,
to bring decency back to the room.

But he also needs encouragement
as he makes his way through life,
because although things may just land in his lap –
there will still be struggle and strife.
Boys have emotions,
males can be sensitive, too.
Men have to vie for attention
in the same way that women do.

It's just that when men shout, they're heard.
And when men fight, they win.
And when men sit at the table –
they don't always let women in.
So I'd like to tell my boy to
be brave and follow his dreams.
But remember the battles his sister will face
and work together; we achieve more in teams.

BUT I WANTED A BABY

When I was a child, I played with dolls
but I wanted my own baby.
As a teenager, I babysat other people's kids
but I wanted my own baby.
(I nearly had one. But I didn't).
When I was twenty-five, I got married and wanted a baby.
But he wasn't ready, so we waited.
I turned twenty-seven, he said he wanted one too.
Soon, we'd have a baby.
I turned twenty-eight. Still no baby.
And then the day I turned twenty-nine, I was in hospital
giving birth to our first baby.
A year later, I turned thirty and our daughter turned one.
I wanted another baby.
He wasn't ready. But then three months later, he was.
It didn't happen. Not until the following spring.
And now our son is one. And I want another.
Not now, but maybe in a year.
People say: you have one of each – you're done.
But that's not how the heart operates.
I wish it was. I wish I could stop here, satisfied.
I want to be present; to enjoy life as it is now.
But I can't stop thinking about having another baby.
He says two's enough. (It probably is.)
He says: after the next, you'll want another.
I know that I won't. Though I don't know how I know.
Because I want another one, I keep thinking:
Do I feel sick because I'm pregnant?
Am I tired because I'm pregnant?
Does my back ache because I'm pregnant?
I know that I'm not. But maybe I'm willing it to happen.
Because if it happened without us planning,
we wouldn't have to make the decision.

And every year that passes takes me closer to the menopause.
But I don't know why they call it a 'pause', because it's not.
It's the end.
And what if I get there, and think:
But I wanted a baby.

ME-TIME

The baby comes everywhere with me:
the dinner table, the sofa, the toilet, the bed.
But not the shower.
So every morning, after a feed,
I mount the stairs for my
quarter-hour of 'me-time'.
A hot shower. Fruity shower gel.
Washed hair. A podcast or music.
Cocoa butter on my dry body and
Nivea on my face.
I piss in peace.
Clean my teeth (again –
I'll have done it once first thing).
Spray Chanel Chance on my throat and wrists
(but not my chest, in case he suckles there).
I dress in a button-down jumpsuit with an
ugly maternity bra hidden underneath.
Beige. Or faded black. Or grey (once white).
My hair is long and knotty.
I release it from the towel turban and
brush it out. Quickly.
Time is running out.
I paint my lips pink or red
and return to my hungry baby.

NEW MOTHERHOOD, ONCE AGAIN

A document of gratitude and love

The hood goes up; I'm a mother, again.
And it's not just me whose role changes:
my mother's a new grandma,
my daughter is now a sister,
my sister is an auntie anew.
My brother – an uncle,
my father a grandpa,
my husband's a new father, too.

Life shifts and twists; I'm a mother, again.
And it reminds me of all that I have:
a mother who nurtures,
a daughter with such tenderness,
a sister who's like my backbone.
A brother enamoured,
a father who dotes,
a husband who puts my needs before his own.

As I sit and reflect on being a mother, again.
I'm so grateful for all that I have:
a mother who is generous,
a daughter full of laughter,
A sister who will always give me time.
A brother cracking jokes,
a father eager and willing,
a husband whose ideals reflect mine.

Because becoming a mother; a mother, again –
makes me feel somewhat vulnerable and in need:
of my mother's love,
of my daughter's forgiveness,
of my sister protecting me.
Of my brother's companionship,
of my father's rational thoughts,
of my husband – with whom I'm safe and yet free.

Annie Ridout is editor-in-chief of digital parenting and lifestyle magazine *The Early Hour*, a freelance journalist (*Guardian*, *Stylist*, *Red*, *Metro*), author of *The Freelance Mum: A flexible career guide for better work-life* and runs online courses for freelancers and business owners. She lives in London with her husband and their three children – aged five, two and eight weeks. This is her first collection of poetry.

Website: annieridout.com
Instagram: @annieridout
Twitter: @annieridout

COLOPHON

Design: Matt Bucknall
Photo: Penny Wincer

annieridout.com

First Edition
Published by Annie Ridout Ltd © 2019